# A TWIST IN TWENTIES

## DHEERAJ MOHAN

Copyright © Dheeraj Mohan
All Rights Reserved.

This book has been self-published with all reasonable efforts taken to make the material error-free by the author. No part of this book shall be used, reproduced in any manner whatsoever without written permission from the author, except in the case of brief quotations embodied in critical articles and reviews.

The Author of this book is solely responsible and liable for its content including but not limited to the views, representations, descriptions, statements, information, opinions and references ["Content"]. The Content of this book shall not constitute or be construed or deemed to reflect the opinion or expression of the Publisher or Editor. Neither the Publisher nor Editor endorse or approve the Content of this book or guarantee the reliability, accuracy or completeness of the Content published herein and do not make any representations or warranties of any kind, express or implied, including but not limited to the implied warranties of merchantability, fitness for a particular purpose. The Publisher and Editor shall not be liable whatsoever for any errors, omissions, whether such errors or omissions result from negligence, accident, or any other cause or claims for loss or damages of any kind, including without limitation, indirect or consequential loss or damage arising out of use, inability to use, or about the reliability, accuracy or sufficiency of the information contained in this book.

Made with ♥ on the Notion Press Platform
www.notionpress.com

This book is dedicated to my mother's fighting spirit and Lord Krishna's invisible guidance that makes me perform my duties.

# Contents

# Contents

# Contents

# Contents

# Contents

# Introduction

In a completely metamorphosed world of the new millennial, complex and twisted human nature is subtly showcased inthese stories.

# Preface

The stories depict in just twenty words the shades and shenanigans of
human follies, fixations, and fascinations, with a twist.

# About The Author

Dheeraj Mohan, a seeker, dreamer, and learner at heart is an entertainment and media professional, screenwriter, poet and an author.

# ONE
## MASSIVE QUAKE

He predicted massive earthquake on a particular day. Nothing happened. But he suffered a heart attack as his prediction failed.

# TWO

## BOOMERANG

He was authorized to tap certain phone numbers. Eventually he was shunted by his boss for snooping on him too.

# THREE

## DOSSIER

He lambasted his adversary and vowed his arrest. He couldn't do it as the adversary had a dossier on him.

# FOUR
## TOXIC TALES

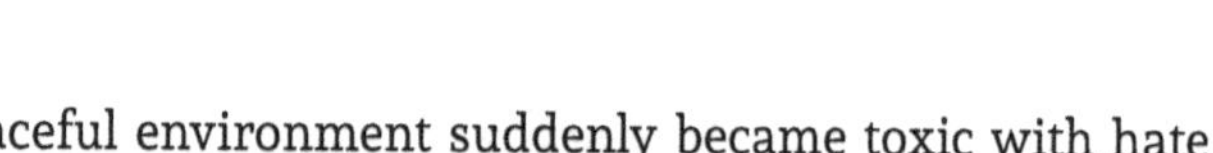

A peaceful environment suddenly became toxic with hate speeches. Ruling party realised to win elections, atmosphere had to be vitiated.

# FIVE

## OVERKILL

Ruling establishment poured in all its resources to win a particular state's elections. This very overkill sounded its death knell.

# SIX

## EXPOSURE

The producer cheated her of her share. She went ahead to expose the porn film racket run by his company.

# SEVEN

## DIVORCE DUEL

Her cousin seduced her husband. So, she got her divorce with a massive settlement. She shared it with her cousin.

# EIGHT

## ENVY

His rocketing career made quite a few jealous. They trapped him in his maid's rape case and ruined his career

# NINE

## MASKED IDENTITY

She being the daughter of his best friend, was launched in his film. In fact she was his own daughter.

# TEN

## RETRIBUTION

Unable to fit in films she switched careers. As an IPS officer she hauled movie bigwigs for casting couch rackets.

# ELEVEN

## PROMISE

He assured her that he will surely return but was martyred in war. She died during childbirth delivering a boy..

# TWELVE

## ROBE OF HONOR

He always felt pride and honor to hold the national flag. One day his mortal remains came wrapped in it.

# THIRTEEN

## GALLANT GESTURE

He declined the gallantry award and recommended his junior's name instead, who had saved his life by taking the bullet.

# FOURTEEN

## Backyard Skeletons

Home Minister gave strict orders to find the hate-speech monger, who had mysteriously taken shelter in his own backyard only.

# FIFTEEN

## SPLIT PERSONALITY

Top cop exhorted the victims to lodge FIRs against the faceless extortion kingpin, who unknown to him was himself alone!

# SIXTEEN
## DOUBLE EDGE

He used his affair with his heroine to attract young men, who were her admirers, with intention to seduce them.

# SEVENTEEN

## COMMITMENT

A committed supporter of a political ideology shifted to a rival party. He said his principle of commitment was intact.

# EIGHTEEN

## PAYBACK

He fled the country to avoid bloodshed. But was assassinated by his aides for having left people high and dry.

# NINETEEN

## HEAD AND TAIL

He credited his lucky stars when he became the President. And then arrested the astrologer who predicted his inevitable ouster.

# TWENTY

## In Vain

After a coup the rich and mighty scrambled to leave. They couldn't as the militia sealed off all the ports.

# TWENTY-ONE
## LOST CAUSE

He vowed that if she left him for someone else, he will still never forget her. Then he developed Alzheimer's.

# TWENTY-TWO
## HOMELESS

He constructed a mansion for his family. After housewarming ceremonies all had to flee as there was a bloody coup.

# TWENTY-THREE

## DREAM COME TRUE

In desperation he clung to the aircraft's wing and fell to his death. His dream of flying though was fulfilled.

# TWENTY-FOUR

## QUAKY PREDICTION

A renowned astrologer predicted a massive earthquake in the Capital. He perished in the quake that instead rocked his hometown.

# TWENTY-FIVE
## PANIC PANGS

It was a bloodless coup in the country. Still more people died of sheer panic than the bullets or bombs.

# TWENTY-SIX
## CEASEFIRE

Media sensationally reported CBI, ED, IT raids on his premises. But suddenly all went quiet. He joined the ruling establishment.

# TWENTY-SEVEN

## LAUNDRY SERVICE

He laundered abroad the borrowed money and after years of litigation returned it. Interest earned was enough for his lifetime.

# TWENTY-EIGHT
## OUT OF SIGHT

He loved a photo-op and any platform for publicity. He loved to see himself glorified. Then he lost his eyesight.

# TWENTY-NINE

## FREEDOM FORTIFIED

The incoming government announced freedom of speech, expression and dissent. For this it constituted a department to regulate and monitor.

# THIRTY

## CHICKENING OUT

He assured his countrymen of protection from the marauding rebels. On first opportunity he managed for himself a safe escape.

# THIRTY-ONE

## MEDIA MANAGEMENT

He launched a brazen media trial against the top cop, to distract viewers from a probe into his own misdemeanors.

# THIRTY-TWO

## GHOST JUDGEMENT

He was accused of being involved in abetting his wife's suicide. But her spirit orchestrated events to prove his innocence.

# THIRTY-THREE
## EMBEDDED ASTROLOGERS

Independent astrologers predicting events, with a subtle chorus of invincibility of the country's PM, turned out to be embedded astrologers.

# THIRTY-FOUR

## ARAB SPRING RELOADED

Media outlets were under government's supervision. Still, it lost the elections as it couldn't control the anti-wave on social media.

# THIRTY-FIVE
## SECURITY SHIELD

The establishment justified every unconstitutional step as protection of national security. Till these became a threat to national security itself.

# THIRTY-SIX

## PULLING OUT A JOKER

It failed to anticipate the developing events, so the ruling establishment played its card of looming war at the border.

# THIRTY-SEVEN
## FAITH SHIELD

At a religious place the devotees did not wear masks even at the peak of the pandemic.

Faith was enough.

# THIRTY-EIGHT

## EXCEPTION

Majority of astrologers with an exception of one, predicted the PM's retirement at his own will. The exception proved right.

# THIRTY-NINE

## DIE-HARD DEVOTION

The Godmans' devotees considered him above reproach. Under that hypnotic perception and spell, he got away with his nefarious deeds.

# FORTY

## REVERSE ENGINEERING

Gradually many experienced veteran leaders left the party and joined the ruling elite. The party had masterminded the defections itself.

# FORTY-ONE

## COOL POOL

In the sultry weather water's feel was soothing. He dived into the pool and woke up. His hut was flooded.

# FORTY-TWO
## Hi Five

When trusted aide made objectionable comments against the high command, he was removed. The high command itself had exhorted him .

# FORTY-THREE

## ET TU

It was imminent that the truth about the scam was to be revealed by the insiders. They all died mysteriously.

# FORTY-FOUR

## BONDS OF BLOOD

She tied Rakhi on her brother's wrist and promised him protection. Then she went on to expose her powerful husband.

# FORTY-FIVE
## INVISIBLE HAND

More than their lives they had the desire to protect their religion's holy book. Mysteriously they reached their homeland safely.

# FORTY-SIX

## SANCTITY ON SALE

The holy book was brought back from abroad with reverence. At home the Minister found nothing but photo-op in it.

# FORTY-SEVEN
## HUSH HUSH WISH

She considered his home like her own maternal home and his mother as her own. Then she became her daughter-in-law.

# FORTY-EIGHT

## MASQUERADE

People teased him by taking name of the Lord he abhorred.
Inside he was happy they somehow took HIS name.

# FORTY-NINE

## TURN OF THE WHEEL

Overnight their life turned topsy turvy due to overthrow of the government. Now they were amongst the new ruling elite.

# FIFTY

## REPERCUSSIONS

He was nonchalant about purveying porn content. But was devastated when his son and daughter were taunted by their schoolmates.

# FIFTY-ONE
## NURSING GAMES

She had gone to nurse her ailing sister who passed away.
She stayed back for life after marrying her brother-in-law.

# FIFTY-TWO

## DECEPTIVE APPEARANCE

In every senior citizen queue, he was being turned away. He had recently turned sixty but looked in his forties.

# FIFTY-THREE

## KARMA

As a spokesperson of ruling elite, he made very many derogatory statements. The power equation changed. He was lynched publicly.

# FIFTY-FOUR

## 'LEMON'ADE

The government scrambled to evacuate countrymen from the neighboring country. Then spent millions to publicize that it was thoroughly prepared.

# FIFTY-FIVE
## SUFFOCATING KNOT

He was besotted with the famous actress and married her. After marriage he was miserable for her being so famous.

# FIFTY-SIX
## BATCH-CATCH

As director of the country's top investigation agency, he exposed his batchmate handling national security, for being a double agent.

# FIFTY-SEVEN

## Changing Fortunes

She dumped him and married his friend for power pretige and security, who later got arrested for corruption and extortion.

# FIFTY-EIGHT
## Taking No Chances

He was known for his integrity. He got hold of an explosive information about a top politician. He dunked it.

# FIFTY-NINE

## IMAGE

His poetry and verses were suffused with views against injustice, corruption, and immorality. His private life was full of debauchery.

# SIXTY

## BROKEN PROMISES

He wanted reasonable money for himself and vowed to donate the rest. He forgot his vow and turned a pauper.

# SIXTY-ONE
## VEXING VACCINE

He exhorted the public to get vaccinated. By the time majority was vaccinated he expired without having a jab himself.

# SIXTY-TWO
## CRASH LANDING

To escape torture and death at the hands of a terror regime they fled and perished in an air crash.

# SIXTY-THREE

## PAYBACK

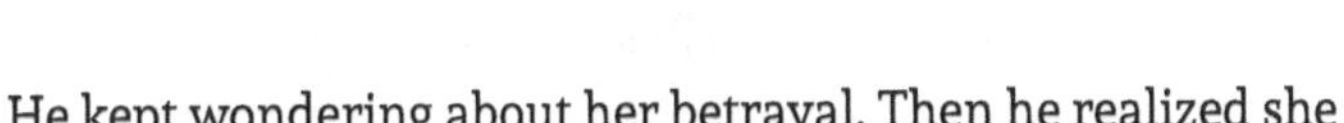

He kept wondering about her betrayal. Then he realized she was his partner in previous life whom he had cheated.

# SIXTY-FOUR
## Vaccine Exclusive

A unique exclusive club emerged. Its exclusivity was derived not by the efficacy but by the price of the vaccine.

# SIXTY-FIVE

## NEIGHBOR INDEED

The neighboring country's turmoil was a blessing for the ruling elite. It shifted the focus from its own gross incompetence.

# SIXTY-SIX

## PUFFED UP

The hosts lavishly praised the victory of the visiting team. In the decider the visitors were mauled by the hosts.

# SIXTY-SEVEN

## AT YOUR SERVICE

He was dismissed from civil services at the Court's intervention for not upholding the Constitution, but peddling an ideological agenda.

# SIXTY-EIGHT

## ME POWERED

She was denied her conjugal rights. She filed a case against her husband. The Courts got perplexed at this role-reversal.

# SIXTY-NINE

## MURDER
## ASSURANCE

Husband received crores in insurance claim on her wife's 'accidental' death. Loads of moolah distributed to hush up the murder.

# SEVENTY

## DIFFERENT STROKES

She was willing to leave her home and lineage for him. Instead, he married her mother for wealth and connections.

# SEVENTY-ONE
## NO ESCAPE

On Janmashtami he vowed that henceforth he will not worship Lord Krishna. In dreams he was playing pranks with Him.

# SEVENTY-TWO

## FINDING PURPOSE

Aimless, he was desperate to commit suicide. He spotted a drowning baby and rushed for rescue. He found his purpose.

# SEVENTY-THREE
## YOURS TRULY

Though he was a legend and very arrogant, he learnt lessons in humility, while spotting talent and hearing underdog stories.

# SEVENTY-FOUR
## TERROR TAIL

The ruling establishment was losing its popularity. A neighboring country's coup gave it a favorite horse of terrorism to flog.

# SEVENTY-FIVE
## STARS ON SALE

The movie was mediocre but was given four to five stars rating, across the 'unbiased' media, that was suitably compensated.

# SEVENTY-SIX
## BACKYARD

Top cop's son was arrested for carrying drugs. He named the kingpin. It turned out to be his own father.

# SEVENTY-SEVEN
## BOBBITT

He was relentless in his pursuit to get her. Eventually under pressure she married him and then did his Bobbitt.

# SEVENTY-EIGHT

## MADE-UP RELATIONSHIP

During chatting late at night, he suddenly asked for her selfie. She refused point blank. As she was without make-up.

# SEVENTY-NINE

## LAST RESORT

He married for her fame. She married him on the rebound. Divorce was inevitable in this most hyped celebrity wedding.

# EIGHTY

## BELITTLED

His party was predicted to lose but swept the polls. Media houses were exposed for running paid campaigns against it.

# EIGHTY-ONE
## TOY OH BOY!

She got married to a boy whom she liked. She was happy. Mother was happy too to have her toy-boy.

# EIGHTY-TWO
## EASY MONEY

She vowed that she would quit escort service once her financial difficulties got over. Then she started loving to serve.

# EIGHTY-THREE
## BEING FAITHFUL

When she ended the relationship, he reasoned she couldn't be faithful to her husband, how could she be to him.

# EIGHTY-FOUR
## CRASH LANDING

He was flying with full security intact. There was no threat to his life. His pilot crashed the helicopter deliberately.

# EIGHTY-FIVE

## GHOSTLY REVENGE

After perishing in an air crash his name was incorrectly spelled across the media platforms. So, his ghost took revenge.

# EIGHTY-SIX

## BLAME GAME

The colleague who arrested him for escorting a banned outfit's operative, was transferred for spoiling the game of the Deep-State.

# EIGHTY-SEVEN
## ACHILLES HEEL

His image was invincible. No one could dislodge him. Then suddenly his trusted lieutenants started dying. His position became vulnerable.

# EIGHTY-EIGHT
## BEWITCHED

She was ridiculed for marrying a dark-skinned young man. But she felt she saw her loving Lord Krishna in him.

# EIGHTY-NINE

## IRONY

Astrologers doubted his becoming the head-of -government. He swept the polls, but before swearing-in ceremony died of a massive heart attack.

# NINETY

# THE BENEVOLENT EARTH

He purchased a piece of land with his meagre pension fund. Digging up for foundations he struck a buried treasure.

# NINETY-ONE
## DEFLECTION

He was relentless to expose the corruption of his rivals. This was his strategy to deflect attention from his own.

# NINETY-TWO

## SPIRITED LEADERSHIP

She was lauded for her indefatigable spirit in managing the whole company. She said she was guided by a spirit.

# NINETY-THREE

## ALLIANCE

Regarding the two smaller states the staunch rivals had a deal. For a larger state they fought tooth and nail.

# NINETY-FOUR
## DEAL

He told the media that he resigned voluntarily his captaincy though he was removed. The deal was worth 100 crores.

# NINETY-FIVE
## MARTYRDOM

He wanted to escape as his life was in danger. But he was trapped. He then played the martyr's card.

# NINETY-SIX
## GRADUATION

As a medical student she was forced to serve in a war-torn country. She returned home to a hero's welcome.

# NINETY-SEVEN
## DISPATCHED

As a war correspondent his dispatches and reports were eagerly followed. Then one day report of his body-bag was dispatched.

# NINETY-EIGHT

## BORN AGAIN

Her husband died in an ambush. That very day she went into labor and gave birth to a baby boy.

# NINETY-NINE
## NO ESCAPE

To escape the eventual siege, they left the city for a safer place. Their car overturned leaving them all dead.

# ONE HUNDRED

## PREMONITION

Non-stop barking made him get out and walk his dog. Soon after, his apartment block was hit by a missile.

www.ingramcontent.com/pod-product-compliance
Lightning Source LLC
Chambersburg PA
CBHW021228130726
47988CB00002B/871